# KANSAS

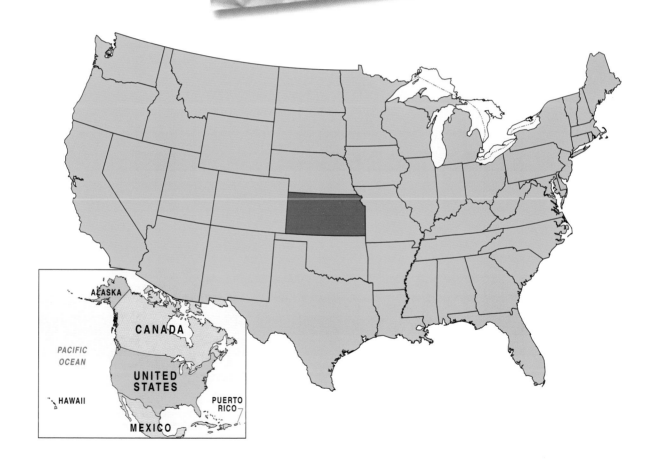

# KANSAS

HELLO
U.S.A.

by Charles Fredeen

Lerner Publications Company

*You'll find this picture of a sunflower at the beginning of each chapter in this book. Kansans once considered the sunflower a weed, but by 1903 they had made it their official state flower. The large and hardy yellow flower appears on the state's flag and seal, as well as in fields all over the state.*

Cover (left): Combine harvesting wheat near Winfield. Cover (right): Cowboy on bucking bronco, Hutchinson. Pages 2-3: School in Tallgrass Prairie National Preserve, Strong City. Page 3: Prairie dogs.

Copyright © 2002 by Lerner Publications Company

*This book is available in two editions:*
Library binding by Lerner Publications Company, a division of Lerner Publishing Group
Soft cover by First Avenue Editions, an imprint of Lerner Publishing Group
241 First Avenue North
Minneapolis, MN 55401 U.S.A.

Website address: www.lernerbooks.com


Library of Congress Cataloging-in-Publication Data

Fredeen, Charles, 1956–
     Kansas / by Charles Fredeen (Rev. and expanded 2nd ed.)
        p.   cm. — (Hello U.S.A.)
     Includes index.
Summary: Introduces the history, geography, people, industries, and other highlights of Kansas.
     ISBN 0-8225-4082-7 (lib. bd. : alk. paper)
     ISBN 0-8225-0780-3 (pbk. : alk. paper)
     1. Kansas—Juvenile literature. [1. Kansas.] I. Title. II. Series.
     F681.3.F74 2002
     978.1—dc21                                                    2001006220

Manufactured in the United States of America
1  2  3  4  5  6  –  JR  –  07  06  05  04  03  02

# CONTENTS

Grassy plains stretch across most of Kansas.

# THE LAND

## The Sunflower State

**P**lains overflowing with tall prairie grass as far as the eye can see. Fields bursting with big yellow sunflowers. Blue skies sometimes darkened by a twister or a blinding dust storm. All of this, and much more, is Kansas.

Kansas is a midwestern state. It sits exactly in the center of the U.S. mainland. Shaped like a rectangle, Kansas borders Nebraska in the north, Missouri in the east, Oklahoma in the south, and Colorado in the west. Kansas is often called the Breadbasket of America, since it is the major provider of wheat, one of the nation's most important foods.

Sunflowers brighten this Kansas field.

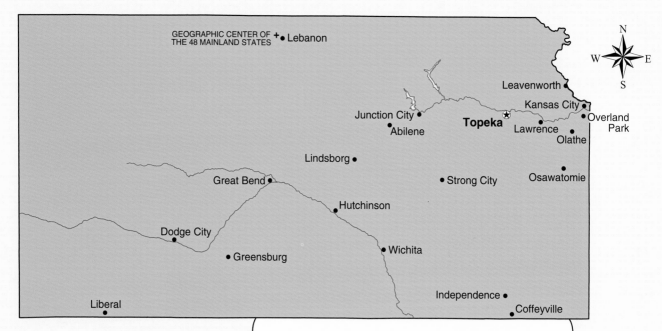

GEOGRAPHIC CENTER OF
THE 48 MAINLAND STATES ✛● Lebanon

Leavenworth ●

Kansas City ●

Junction City ● **Topeka** ★ Overland Park ●

Abilene ● Lawrence ●

Olathe ●

Lindsborg ●

Osawatomie ●

Great Bend ● ● Strong City

Hutchinson ●

Dodge City ● ● Wichita

● Greensburg

Independence ●

Liberal ● Coffeyville ●

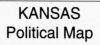

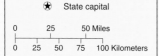

**KANSAS**
**Political Map**

★ State capital

0      25      50 Miles

0   25   50   75   100 Kilometers

The drawing of Kansas on this page is called a political map. It shows features created by people, including cities, railways, and parks. The map on the facing page is called a physical map. It shows physical features of Kansas, such as, mountains, rivers, and lakes. The colors represent a range of elevations, or heights above sea level (see legend box). This map also shows the geographical regions of Kansas.

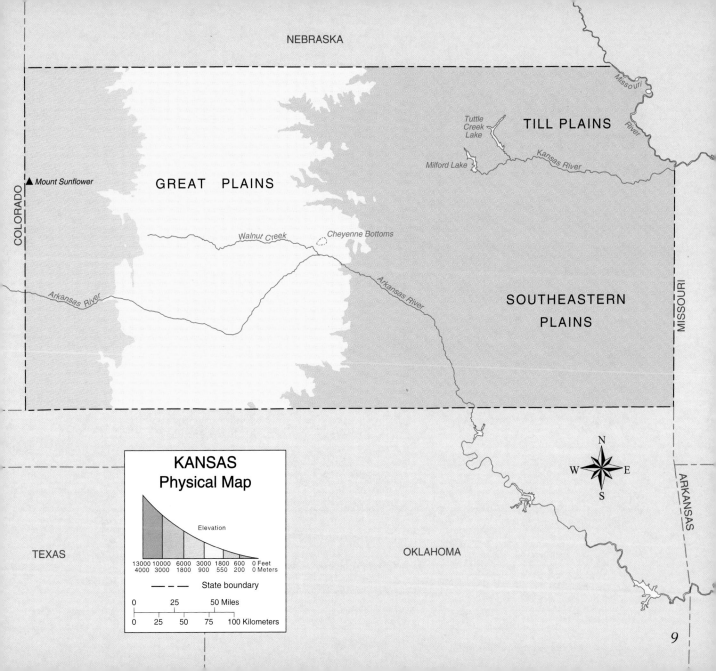

NEBRASKA

MISSOURI

TILL PLAINS

Tuttle
Creek
Lake

Milford Lake

Kansas River

COLORADO

▲ Mount Sunflower

GREAT    PLAINS

Walnut Creek

Cheyenne Bottoms

Arkansas River

Arkansas River

SOUTHEASTERN
PLAINS

MISSOURI

ARKANSAS

N
W        E
S

KANSAS
Physical Map

Elevation

| 13000 | 10000 | 6000 | 3000 | 1800 | 600 | 0 Feet |
| 4000 | 3000 | 1800 | 900 | 550 | 200 | 0 Meters |

- - -     State boundary

0        25        50 Miles

0    25    50    75    100 Kilometers

TEXAS

OKLAHOMA

9

These wheat kernels, or seeds, will be ground into flour and used to make bread or other food products.

Much of the state's wheat is grown in the Great Plains region, which stretches across central and western Kansas. Most of the Great Plains look flat, but the region actually slopes upward toward Colorado. The region reaches its greatest height in the west, at a place called Mount Sunflower. Mount Sunflower, which is not actually a mountain peak but a small hill, is 4,039 feet above sea level.

Eastern Kansas is divided into two geographic regions—the Till Plains and the Southeastern Plains.

**Glaciers,** huge sheets of ice formed in prehistoric times, slowly moved over northeastern Kansas to create the region known as the Till Plains. The glaciers left deposits of **till,** or crushed rocks and dirt, which formed a rich soil. Thousands of years ago, strong dust storms carried some of this soil westward, enriching the Great Plains.

At Monument Rocks in western Kansas, many fossils are buried deep within the rocks.

The Southeastern Plains cover southeastern Kansas. The area has **prairies** (grasslands), rolling hills, flatlands, limestone ridges, and pockets of dense forest. Farmers have taken advantage of the

Wildflowers, like these asters *(above),* bloom throughout Kansas. About 200 kinds of prairie grasses *(right)* grow in Kansas.

flatlands in the region by covering them with crops. A tall, reddish brown grass called bluestem waves gently in the wind over large sections of the Southeastern Plains. Cows and sheep graze on this grass.

Three major rivers flow through the state. They are the Kansas River (also known as the Kaw), the Missouri River, and the Arkansas River. The Kansas River flows eastward and eventually empties into the Missouri River, which forms part of the northeastern border of the state. The Arkansas River winds through southern Kansas, then crosses Oklahoma and Arkansas to meet the Mississippi River. Parts of the Arkansas dry up for most of the year because people use so much of its water for irrigation.

Most of the large lakes in Kansas are artificial. These lakes, called **reservoirs,** were created when dams were built to store river water. The reservoirs have become popular for boating, swimming, and other water sports. Milford Lake and Tuttle Creek Lake are among the biggest reservoirs in Kansas.

The branches of a bush hang heavy with ice after a winter storm.

The state's weather varies widely from season to season. During the summer, temperatures average 74° F but sometimes pass 100° F. Winter temperatures, on the other hand, average about 30° F and have dropped below 0° F.

Kansas receives about 27 inches of rain and snow each year, with the most falling on the Southeastern Plains. Throughout Kansas, winter blizzards, spring tornadoes, and summer thunderstorms and dust storms can appear suddenly, threatening the landscape. Occasionally, mild earthquakes shake the ground.

**Droughts,** or long periods of little or no rainfall, also occur in Kansas. Droughts leave crops thirsty for water. They also leave the soil dry and loose for the wind to pick up and shoot across the plains in blinding clouds of dust.

In the summer, storm clouds sometimes fill the Kansas sky.

Shade is hard to find in Kansas. Few forests shelter the land because trees, which need a lot of water, have not survived the state's frequent droughts. Only about 3 percent of the state is forestland. But several kinds of trees, such as cottonwood, maple, ash, pecan, willow, and black walnut, grow in Kansas.

Nearly 200 types of grasses blanket the prairies of Kansas. These kinds of plants fed the millions of buffalo that once thundered across the Great Plains. Most of the buffalo were killed for their hides or for sport in the 1800s. Only about 600 buffalo live in Kansas, and all are located on game preserves, where the animals are protected from hunters.

The most common wild animals in Kansas include pheasants, coyotes, white-tailed deer, and foxes. Scurrying prairie dogs burrow into the ground, while rabbits hop through the grasses.

Ring-necked pheasant

# THE HISTORY

## The Wild West

Kansas's history is filled with tales of fierce battles, shifty lawmakers, gunfights, and murder. For a time, the state was even known as "Bleeding Kansas." Much of the trouble took place after the arrival of white settlers. But the state's history goes back a long way—long before Kansas even got its name.

About 10,000 years ago, Native Americans, or Indians, came to the central part of North America. This area includes the land that later became Kansas.

The Kaw Indians lived in villages along the Kansas River.

Some Plains Indian tribes built houses of earth or straw.

These prehistoric Indians were hunters. They also ate roots and plant foods. Around A.D. 1000, the Indians began planting and harvesting crops. Eventually, the Indian groups in the region became known as the Plains Indians.

One Plains Indian nation was the Kaw, or Kansa. Their name means "people of the south wind." The state of Kansas was named after the Kaw.

The Kaw lived in eastern Kansas along a river called the Kansas. For homes, they built earthen lodges that were owned by the women of the group. Kaw women also took charge of sacred burials and oversaw the farming.

Kaw men were hunters. The Kaw used bows and arrows to kill buffalo, their main target. The entire animal was used. The meat was eaten, and the hide became clothing and blankets. The Kaw carved the bones and horns into tools and jewelry.

The Osage, another Plains Indian nation, lived in southeastern Kansas, where game was plentiful. Thousands of buffalo grazed on the area's bluestem grasses. The Pawnee Indians lived in earthen lodges along the Arkansas River. They were highly skilled farmers. The Wichita Indians also lived along the Arkansas River. Wichita homes were made of grass.

Each nation had its own customs, but the nations also shared many traditions. Most of the Plains Indians farmed and hunted. Warriors often belonged to military groups. All the nations held ceremonies in which they asked their gods for success in hunting, in marriage, and in battle.

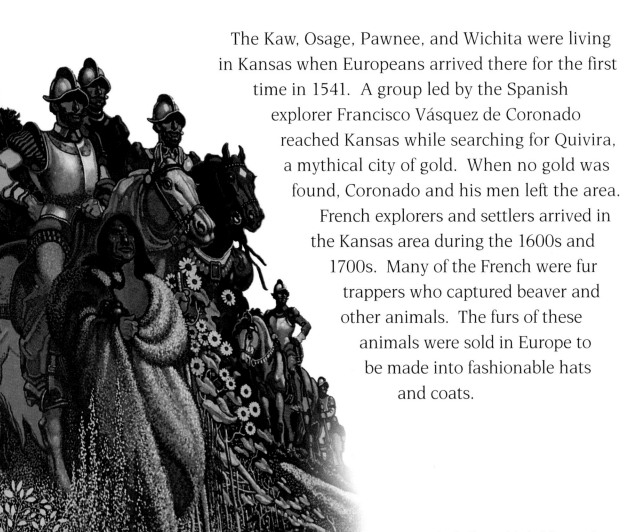

The Kaw, Osage, Pawnee, and Wichita were living in Kansas when Europeans arrived there for the first time in 1541. A group led by the Spanish explorer Francisco Vásquez de Coronado reached Kansas while searching for Quivira, a mythical city of gold. When no gold was found, Coronado and his men left the area. French explorers and settlers arrived in the Kansas area during the 1600s and 1700s. Many of the French were fur trappers who captured beaver and other animals. The furs of these animals were sold in Europe to be made into fashionable hats and coats.

An Indian guide led Coronado and his soldiers through what later became Kansas.

# Horses and the Great Plains

Horses were brought to North America from Spain by explorers in the 1600s. The arrival of these animals changed the lifestyles of many Native Americans. On horseback, Indians were able to travel great distances in short periods of time, carrying their belongings with them.

During the 1600s, horses brought more Indian groups to Kansas. The Arapaho, Cheyenne, and Comanche were among the many tribes that rode on horseback from the north and the south onto the Great Plains. These Indians probably left their homelands in search of sources of food or to escape their enemies.

Probably most important was that horses changed the way the Plains Indians hunted. Instead of stalking their prey on foot, hunters could ride alongside a herd of buffalo. Some groups of Plains Indians left their crops and villages to follow buffalo westward across the Great Plains.

When early settlers entered Kansas, miles of open prairie stretched before them.

Before long, the French claimed a large area of what became the central United States. They called their territory Louisiana. In 1803 France sold the Louisiana Territory to the recently formed United States. This deal, called the Louisiana Purchase, included the area that became Kansas.

The U.S. government was eager to map the land it had bought. Two army officers, Captain Meriwether Lewis and Lieutenant William Clark, were chosen to lead the mapping expedition. They passed through Kansas in June of 1804.

Lewis and Clark were not impressed by what they saw in Kansas. They thought the large expanse of dry grassland was of little use to the United States. Explorers who arrived later also thought the area was unfit for settlement.

Government officials agreed with the explorers but still had plans for the area. Many Native Americans on the East Coast had been forced off their homelands by European settlers, and the U.S. government had promised to give the Indians land in another area. Between 1825 and 1842, about 30 eastern Indian nations were ordered to move to Kansas.

Meriwether Lewis *(top)* and William Clark *(bottom)*

Many pioneers traveled across Kansas on the Oregon Trail *(above)*. In 1853 Fort Riley *(above right)* was built as a U.S. cavalry post. The fort was also a rest stop for travelers and a supply store for Indians and settlers.

At about the same time, large numbers of pioneers were heading west, looking for land on which to plant crops and raise livestock. Traveling on paths such as the Oregon and Santa Fe Trails, these people only passed through Kansas, which still belonged to the Indians.

In 1854 Congress passed the Kansas-Nebraska Act. This law made Kansas and Nebraska U.S. territories and opened them up to white settlers. The act also let Kansas and Nebraska decide whether to allow slavery within their borders.

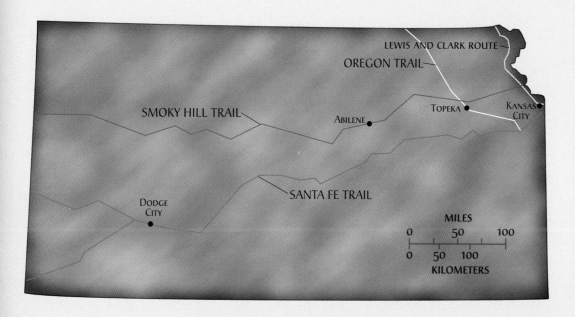

Map labels: LEWIS AND CLARK ROUTE, OREGON TRAIL, SMOKY HILL TRAIL, ABILENE, TOPEKA, KANSAS CITY, SANTA FE TRAIL, DODGE CITY

MILES
0    50    100

0    50    100
KILOMETERS

# Westward Bound

Not long after the Lewis and Clark expedition, Kansas became a crossroads between the East Coast and the West Coast. In 1821 the Santa Fe Trail opened, making trade possible with the Spaniards who lived in what would become the southwestern United States. Most of the route passed through Kansas.

In the early 1840s, large groups of pioneers in covered wagons braved the Oregon Trail. It led settlers from the Midwest farther westward to Oregon and California. The Smoky Hill Trail opened up when gold was discovered in Denver, Colorado.

During the 1850s, the United States was bitterly divided over slavery. The Northern states no longer wanted people to own slaves. The Southern states wanted to continue using slaves. After the Kansas-Nebraska Act was passed, the North and the South each tried to sway Kansas their way. This threw Kansas into a turmoil that would earn it the name Bleeding Kansas.

In 1855 Kansas held an election to decide whether the territory would support slavery. Citizens of

Missouri, a neighboring slave state, poured into Kansas armed with guns. They beat up judges, voted illegally, and won control of the territory's government. After the crooked elections, the territory's new leaders created laws that ordered the death of anyone who helped to free a slave.

John Brown believed slavery was wrong. In 1856 Brown and his followers murdered five men who wanted Kansas to be a slave state. The act sparked more riots in Bleeding Kansas.

People who favored slavery fought those who wanted to end it.  Battles along the Kansas-Missouri border were especially violent.  By 1858 antislavery forces in Kansas were strong enough to overthrow the territory's proslavery leaders.  By 1859 the new government officials had outlawed slavery.  Kansas was admitted to the Union on January 29, 1861, becoming the 34th state and the newest free, or nonslave, state.

Around this time, several Southern states withdrew from the Union and formed the Confederate States, a separate country that allowed slavery.  When Union troops were sent into the South to stop the Confederates, fighting broke out.  The Civil War (1861–1865) had begun.

Few Civil War battles took place in Kansas, but thousands of Kansans lost their lives fighting for the Union army.  Many of the state's soldiers fought in famous battles outside of Kansas.  Most battles actually fought in the state occurred near the end of the war when Confederate, or Southern, troops stormed through eastern Kansas.

# Quantrill Raid

Only a few battles were fought in Kansas during the Civil War. One was the Quantrill raid of 1863. William Clarke Quantrill lived in Lawrence, Kansas. For a time, he earned a living by stealing black slaves and then returning them to their owners for a reward. When the Civil War started, Quantrill joined the Southern, or Confederate, army.

In August 1863, Quantrill led a group of soldiers in an attack on the town of Lawrence. The soldiers burned most of the town and killed about 150 people, most of whom were not soldiers. Horrified, Confederate leaders arrested Quantrill for murder, but he escaped. Quantrill was killed on a raid in Kentucky in 1865.

After the Civil war, thousands of new settlers arrived in Kansas. Many came because of the Homestead Act of 1862. The act offered 160 acres of free land to anyone who was over the age of 21 or the head of a family. Congress passed this law to encourage settlement in the thinly populated western states, which included Kansas. Most of these **homesteaders** were taking a once-in-a-lifetime opportunity to be able to own land.

Homesteaders in Kansas faced many hardships. Surface water was limited, so settlers had to dig deep wells to bring water up from under the ground. Because few trees grew in Kansas, wood was scarce, and settlers had to build houses out of sod. To fuel fires for cooking and heating, homesteaders used prairie grass, sunflower stalks, buffalo chips, and even corncobs.

Many early pioneers lived in sod houses, or "soddies." Soddies kept pioneers warm in the winter and cool in the summer.

Cowboys drove herds of Texas long-horned cattle through the streets of Dodge City during the late 1800s.

During the late 1860s, railroad companies began laying tracks across the United States. Cowboys drove cattle from Texas to train stations in the Midwest, where the livestock could be transported to markets in the East. Several trails used by the cowboys ended in Kansas at Abilene and Dodge City. Before long, these two cow towns became bustling centers for trading and shipping cattle.

In the 1800s, Kansas cow towns such as Dodge City *(below)* were patrolled by the likes of Wyatt Earp *(right)*, Wild Bill Hickok *(center right)*, and Bat Masterson *(far right)*.

## The Wild West

Brawling and drinking cowboys, who wanted to celebrate after weeks on the long, dry cattle trails, streamed through Kansas's cow towns. They gambled in the local saloons and sometimes even shot one another in the streets. Wyatt Earp, James "Wild Bill" Hickok, and William "Bat" Masterson were among the lawmen who were called in to stop the violence in Kansas, a state that belonged to the Wild West.

*31*

A Mennonite farm

Most Kansans, however, were farmers. These people, called sodbusters, cut down prairie grass and replaced it with crops. But raising crops was difficult. With frequent drought in the area, farmers never seemed to have enough water for their fields.

In the 1870s, a Russian religious group called the Mennonites arrived in Kansas. Each settler carried a packet of wheat called Turkey Red. This type of wheat thrived in the dry fields of Kansas, and the state soon earned its title the Breadbasket of America.

More and more pioneers moved to Kansas and forced the Indians out. Bloody battles broke out between Indians and U.S. soldiers. After years of struggling, many of the Indians agreed to leave their homelands and move south to Oklahoma.

The new settlers now had plenty of land on which to grow crops. As methods of farming improved, farmers were also able to increase their crop yields. From the late 1800s to the 1920s, farmers went from using plows pulled by oxen and horses to using tractors with engines. Tractors could complete the work more quickly than plows could, and farmers had time to break more land. The state's crops were so abundant that other states depended on buying extra wheat from Kansas.

The state nearly lost its ability to feed the nation during the Great Depression of the 1930s. People throughout the United States had little money, so farmers had to sell their crops at low prices. Banks closed and people lost their savings. Many Kansans, along with other Americans, found themselves out of work.

A Kansas farmer shows off his healthy corn crop.

The Breadbasket of America suffered even more when a long drought settled on the Midwest. With little or no rainfall, farmland dried up and crops died. Strong winds cut across Kansas, stripping farmland of its fertile soil. Wind carried the soil in clouds of dust that coated everything in their paths. Southwestern Kansas became part of the **Dust Bowl,** an area of the Great Plains that experienced intense dust storms throughout the 1930s.

As the Depression and the dust storms eased in the late 1930s, Kansas slowly recovered. A major boost

Dust clouds filled the Kansas sky and blocked out the sun during the Dust Bowl days of the 1930s.

*Left:* General Eisenhower became a national hero during World War II. *Below:* Oil gushes from a Kansas well.

to the state's economy came during World War II (1939–1945). Kansas was rich in oil and other minerals, as well as in natural gas and helium. All of these resources were needed to keep factories running while the United States was at war overseas.

More than 200,000 Kansans fought in World War II, including General Dwight D. Eisenhower, who was raised in Abilene. Eisenhower gained worldwide attention after planning the invasion of Normandy, a successful military operation that led to the end of the war. He was elected president of the United States in 1952 and served for eight years.

To help their crops grow during droughts, Kansas farmers irrigate, or water, the land.

Modern-day Kansas is a state with many industries and cities as well as farms and rural areas. While the state continues to undergo droughts, Kansans have learned from these hardships. Some farmers use irrigation to keep crops watered, and trees have been planted to hinder dust storms. Conserving soil and water for future generations is a goal throughout the state. These efforts have paid off. In 1990 Kansas produced enough wheat to help save the nation from a food shortage. And in 1998, Kansas farmers raised a record 506 million bushels of wheat.

# PEOPLE & ECONOMY

## Feeding the Nation

The once dust-ridden cow towns of Kansas have been paved in concrete. Cars, not cows, travel down the streets of Abilene and Dodge City, and people live in houses of wood and brick instead of sod. But some things haven't changed. Many Kansans still make a living by working with wheat and beef, just as early settlers did.

Although fewer in number, farmers in Kansas still help to feed the nation. Each year, Kansans grow millions of tons of wheat—more than any other state. Many farmers plant the seeds of Turkey Red wheat, while others grow corn, hay, and soybeans.

Modern Kansans are more likely to be found on bicycles than on horseback.

It took 37 years to build Kansas's state capitol building in Topeka. Kansans wanted the best capitol building their state could afford, and the structure was built in three different stages. Construction began in 1866 and ended in 1903.

Beef cattle graze on ranch land in Kansas.

Each year, farmers and ranchers in Kansas raise more than 6 million head of cattle, which are later sold and butchered. Agriculture—farming and ranching—employs about 6 percent of working Kansans.

Other Kansans process the wheat and beef into food. Flour, which is made from wheat, tops the list of food products made in Kansas, a leading flour-milling state. Workers also pack meat and grind grain into food for livestock.

Farmland covers about 90 percent of Kansas, and farmers plant wheat on much of it. Kansas grows more wheat than any other state.

Most of the light aircraft flown in the United States are made in Kansas. Wichita is well known for the large number of airplanes and helicopters it makes. Other products manufactured in the state are military missiles, railcars and train engines, trailers, and snowplows.

Factory workers put the finishing touches on airplanes.

About 13 percent of Kansas's workers have jobs in factories. But most Kansans—about 60 percent—have service jobs. In this type of work, people help other people or businesses in banks, restaurants, or hospitals. Other service workers sell the flour, beef, airplanes, and railcars made in the state.

Sixteen percent of Kansans have government jobs. Topeka, the capital of Kansas, is home to thousands of government workers. A major U.S. Army base, Fort Leavenworth, is located in the city of Leavenworth. This base, which also houses a prison, provides work for many Kansans.

Service jobs employ more than half of Kansas's workers. This woman works at a cafe along the historic Route 66, a highway created in the 1920s that connected Chicago to Los Angeles.

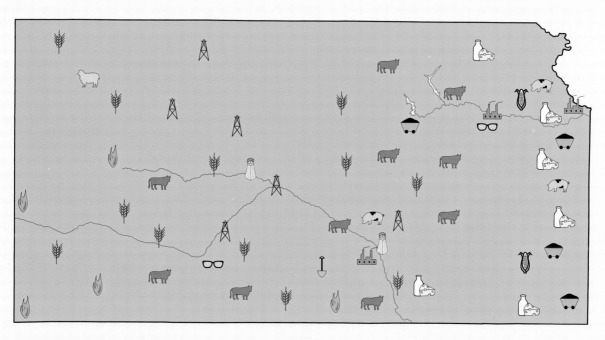

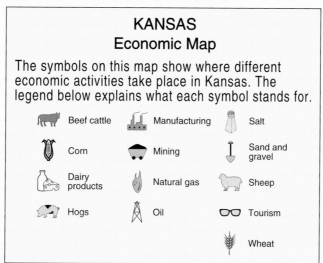

## KANSAS
## Economic Map

The symbols on this map show where different economic activities take place in Kansas. The legend below explains what each symbol stands for.

|  |  |
|--------|---------|
| 🐄 | Beef cattle |
| 🌽 | Corn |
| 🥛 | Dairy products |
| 🐖 | Hogs |
| 🏭 | Manufacturing |
| ⛏ | Mining |
| 🔥 | Natural gas |
| 🛢 | Oil |
| 🧂 | Salt |
| ⚒ | Sand and gravel |
| 🐑 | Sheep |
| 👓 | Tourism |
| 🌾 | Wheat |

This natural gas processing plant is part of Kansas's mining industry.

Minerals are found in most parts of Kansas, and the mining industry employs a small number of the state's workers. A huge salt deposit in Hutchinson yields nearly 45 million tons of salt each year. Oil, which helps fuel U.S. industries, makes a lot of money for Kansas. Other resources include natural gas, coal, limestone, and helium, the gas that keeps balloons afloat.

The population of Kansas is nearly 2.7 million. About 83 percent of Kansans have European ancestors. Latinos make up about 7 percent of the state's population. Six percent of Kansas residents are African American. Kansas also has small numbers of Native Americans and Asian Americans.

About two-thirds of all Kansans live in urban areas. Wichita, Overland Park, and Kansas City are the largest cities in the state, and all three are in the eastern half of the state. Western Kansas is mostly rural, but getting from town to town is easy. Kansas has more miles of highway than most other states.

Both large and small cities in Kansas attract visitors. For Western-art buffs, the Wichita Art Museum has a large collection of Western paintings and sculptures. At the University of Kansas in Lawrence, bug lovers make a beeline for the Snow Entomological Museum, which displays more than 3 million types of insects.

Every other year, Svensk Hyllningsfest in Lindsborg honors Kansas's Swedish pioneers. Here, fiddlers tune their instruments before performing at the festival.

Anyone fascinated with cow towns and gun-slingers will want to stop by Dodge City—known as Cowboy Capital of the World. In this colorful town, visitors can imagine what life was like during the exciting time of Bat Masterson and the Wild West.

Children explore an old train on display in Lawrence.

1073

DONATED IN 1955 BY A.T.&S.F.
RAILROAD IS A 2-6-2 PRAIRIE
TYPE LOCOMOTIVE FROM 1908
1952 IT LOGGED 87184 MILES

Many towns throughout Kansas hold rodeos.

Front Street, Dodge City's main road in the 1870s, has been recreated at Boot Hill Museum. Museums in several Kansas towns hail the expansion of the railroad into the cow towns.

Rodeos also help to keep the traditions of the Wild West alive. Throughout the state, crowds of people cheer as cowboys rope calves, ride bulls and bucking horses, and wrestle steers to the ground. Rodeos are held almost every weekend during the summer months. Horse racing and dog racing bring bettors to the Woodlands racing tracks in Kansas City.

The homes of two famous generals are found in Kansas. General George Armstrong Custer's home still stands at Fort Riley near Junction City. Custer and his cavalry troops were killed by Sioux Indians in 1876 at the Battle of the Little Bighorn in Montana. A museum in Abilene houses the belongings of General Dwight D. Eisenhower.

Kansas has nearly 200 lakes, which people use for fishing and swimming. Some other activities enjoyed in Kansas are hiking along part of the Santa Fe Trail and camping on the prairie. Kansas, in addition to its cities and factories, still has plenty of wide-open countryside.

Large crowds attend Jayhawks basketball games at the University of Kansas.

48

# THE ENVIRONMENT

## Protecting the Wetlands

**E**very spring, people in central Kansas witness something spectacular. Throughout the season, millions of birds that have been flying nonstop for as long as 90 hours land at Cheyenne Bottoms, a 41,000-acre **marshland** near the city of Great Bend. Here, the weary birds find the food, water, and shelter they need before continuing their journey northward.

A flock of geese fills the evening sky.

Cheyenne Bottoms

The birds that arrive at Cheyenne Bottoms are migrating, or moving from one region to another. **Migration** leads some birds southward in the fall. They leave their homes in Canada and the northern United States for places warm enough to supply food, such as berries and insects, during the winter. They return to their nesting areas in the spring, when food there is once again abundant.

Many birds leave the north for the warmer climate of the south when winter strikes.

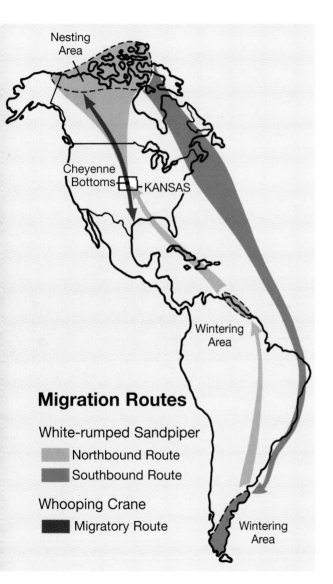

Nesting
Area

Cheyenne
Bottoms⊡ ⊡ KANSAS

Wintering
Area

**Migration Routes**

White-rumped Sandpiper

Northbound Route

Southbound Route

Whooping Crane

Migratory Route

Wintering
Area

Migrating birds follow the same path year after year. Some groups of birds fly southward over the Atlantic Ocean in the fall. When they return in the spring, they follow a different route that takes them over the central United States. About 45 percent of North American shorebirds make Cheyenne Bottoms their first and only stop.

Different kinds of birds follow different migration paths, but once a type of bird chooses a route, the birds travel that path year after year. This chart shows the routes of the white-rumped sandpiper and the endangered whooping crane. Both birds make a stop at Cheyenne Bottoms.

At one time, Kansas had 12 large marshes. Only 4 of these marshes—Quivira, Jamestown, Slate Creek, and Cheyenne Bottoms—remain. The other wetlands dried up naturally or were drained of their water to make room for farms, homes, and businesses.

No one knows why, but migrating birds choose Cheyenne Bottoms as their stopover every spring. If Cheyenne Bottoms dried up, the millions of migrating birds that visit the marshland year after year would lose their place to feed and rest. Because of its importance to migratory birds, Cheyenne Bottoms was designated a Wetlands of International Importance in 1988.

*Top:* Pelicans
*Above:* Lesser yellowlegs

Long-billed dowitchers

Cheyenne Bottoms provides food and nesting areas for nearly half of North America's northbound shorebirds, or wading birds. It becomes a temporary home for 90 percent of certain bird populations, such as the white-rumped sandpiper, the long-billed dowitcher, and the endangered whooping crane. Waterfowl, including ducks and geese, abound.

The water in the Bottoms is generally shallow. The sun reaches the marsh's floor, encouraging plant growth. These plants are important foods for birds and other animals. By using their bills to dig deep into the mud floors, some birds also find beetles, leeches, snails, and worms. Waterfowl feast on fish and frogs. Cattails and other tall marsh plants provide food and shelter.

A yellow-headed blackbird sits among the cattails in a Kansas marsh.

Since the 1940s, Kansans have been keeping the water level in Cheyenne Bottoms desirable for the shorebirds and waterfowl that visit the marsh.

Canals and **dikes** (artificial walls) control the flow of water among several pools within the marsh. When the Bottoms needs more water, it is pumped in from the Arkansas River and from nearby Walnut Creek. Without this extra supply of water, Cheyenne Bottoms would dry up during a drought.

A scientist at Cheyenne Bottoms studies eggs in a duck's nest.

Controlling the level of water in Cheyenne Bottoms, however, is more difficult than it might seem. People, farms, factories, and businesses in Kansas also use the state's water supply, which is limited. When demands on water are heavy, such as during hot, dry summers, the flow of the Arkansas River and of Walnut Creek stops or slows down, and less water is available for Cheyenne Bottoms.

Parts of the Arkansas River dry up for some of the year.

Environmentalists in Kansas want to protect the wildlife habitat available in their state.

Environmentalists study how much water Cheyenne Bottoms loses each year. By learning which areas of the marsh lose the most water and why, Kansans are better able to manage its water supply. Thousands of acres of former wetlands are being restored throughout the state to help enhance existing wetlands. And increased concern has made wetland protection and improvement a priority for Kansans. In 2001, two Kansas environmental groups sued the Environmental Protection Agency, pushing for tougher laws regulating pollution controls on more than 1,000 lakes and streams in the state.

Cheyenne Bottoms is one of the few remaining habitats in the United States for migrating birds. Controlling and protecting its water supply will benefit not only the bird watchers in Great Bend, but also many of North and South America's fine-feathered friends.

## Fun Facts

At the Kansas State University College of Veterinary Medicine, doctors use waterbeds as operating tables for horses.

Dodge City, Kansas, is one of the windiest cities in the United States. Wind speeds average almost 14 miles per hour.

The exact geographic center of the mainland United States is located in Kansas, near the town of Lebanon. For this reason, Kansas is sometimes called the Navel of the Nation.

Kansas claims the world's largest salt deposit. A mine in Hutchinson is large enough to supply the United States with salt for the next 250,000 years.

The world's largest meteorite, a mass of rock and metal from outer space, landed near what later became Greensburg, Kansas, about 2,000 years ago. The meteorite weighed 1,000 pounds.

Susanna Madora Salter was the first woman mayor in the United States. Residents of Argonia, Kansas, elected her to the post in 1887. The election was also the first Kansas city election in which women were allowed to vote.

The geographic center of the mainland United States, located in Lebanon, Kansas, is marked with a brick monument.

# STATE SONG

Kansas's state legislature adopted this popular tune as its state song in 1947.

## HOME ON THE RANGE

*Words by Dr. Brewster Higley; music by Daniel Kelley*

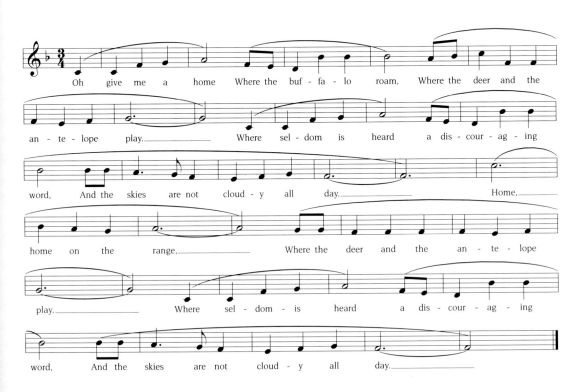

You can hear "Home on the Range" by visiting this website:
<http://www.50states.com/songs/kansas.htm>

# A KANSAS RECIPE

According to legend, 24 Mennonite families from Russia introduced hardy Turkey Red winter wheat to the plains of Kansas in the 1870s. Along with the kernels that they brought overseas, they also brought many tasty recipes. Hemetschwenger, a type of turnover, is one of the many baked goods the Mennonites prepare. This recipe calls for apple filling, but other fruits may be used.

## HEMETSCHWENGER (TURNOVERS)

You will need:

| | |
|---|---|
| 1 cup whipping cream | 4 or 5 tart apples |
| 1 cup butter (softened) | sugar |
| 2 cups flour | cinnamon |

1. Mix whipping cream and butter until blended.
2. Add flour. Mix until dough can be formed into a ball. (Don't overwork it.)
3. Divide dough into two halves to make it easier to roll. Roll each half into a 12-inch square.
4. Cut each half into 9 squares. Each square should be 4 inches by 4 inches.
5. Chop apples into ¼-inch pieces and season with sugar and cinnamon.
6. Place a spoonful of fruit in center of each square. Fold pastry edges over into triangles. Press the sides shut.
7. Prick top of each turnover with a fork for ventilation.
8. Bake turnovers on a cookie sheet at 350° F for 25–30 minutes.
9. Roll hemetschwenger in sugar and cinnamon while warm. Makes 18 turnovers.

# HISTORICAL TIMELINE

**8,000 B.C.**    Native Americans arrive in the area that later became Kansas.

**A.D. 1000**    Native Americans living in the Kansas region begin growing crops.

**1541**    Spanish explorer Francisco Vasquez de Coronado reaches Kansas while searching for gold.

**1700s**    French fur trappers settle in the northeastern corner of the Kansas region.

**1803**    The United States gets Kansas as part of the Louisiana Purchase.

**1821**    The Santa Fe Trail is established, crossing through a large part of Kansas.

**1825–42**    Native American nations, after giving up their eastern lands to the U.S. government, are moved to Kansas.

**1850s**    Violence breaks out in Kansas between antislavery and proslavery groups. The territory is nicknamed "Bleeding Kansas."

**1854**    Congress passes the Kansas-Nebraska Act, opening the territory to white settlers.

**1861**  Kansas becomes the 34th state.

**1863**  William Clarke Quantrill leads a Confederate raid against the town of Lawrence, Kansas.

**1874**  Russian Mennonites introduce Turkey Red wheat to Kansas.

**1930s**  Kansas farmland is damaged by severe dust storms.

**1944**  Dwight D. Eisenhower, from Abilene, leads the Normandy invasion in World War II (1939–1945).

**1990**  Kansas farmers produce 425 million bushels of wheat, helping to save the nation from a food shortage.

**1996**  Kansas senator Bob Dole retires as the longest-serving majority leader in the U.S. Senate.

**1998**  Kansas farmers produce a record 506 million bushels of wheat.

**2001**  Kansas school officials vote to include the theory of evolution in state education standards.

# OUTSTANDING KANSANS

**Kirstie Alley**

**Hugh Beaumont**

**Gwendolyn Brooks**

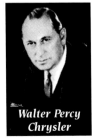

**Walter Percy Chrysler**

**Kirstie Alley** (born 1955), an actress from Wichita, has starred in the television series *Cheers* and *Veronica's Closet.* Alley has also starred in several films, including *Look Who's Talking* and *Drop Dead Gorgeous.*

**Hugh Beaumont** (1909–1982) was better known as Ward Cleaver, father of Beaver on the popular television show *Leave It to Beaver,* which aired from 1957 to 1963. Beaumont was born in Lawrence, Kansas.

**Gwendolyn Brooks** (1917–2000), from Topeka, was the first African American author to win the Pulitzer Prize. She received the award in 1949 for her collection of poems entitled *Annie Allen.* In 1989 she received a lifetime achievement award from the National Endowment for the Arts.

**Walter Percy Chrysler** (1875–1940), born in Wamego, Kansas, was a successful auto manufacturer. He was president of Buick Motor Company from 1916 to 1919 and founded the Chrysler Corporation in 1925.

**William "Buffalo Bill" Cody** (1846–1917) began working in Kansas territory as a messenger for the Pony Express. During the Civil War, he was a scout at Fort Ellsworth. Later he organized a Wild West exhibition that became popular across the nation and abroad.

**John Steuart Curry** (1897–1946) was a painter from Dunavant, Kansas, who painted the regions where he lived. Some of his murals can be seen on the walls of the Kansas state capitol building.

**Charles Curtis** (1860–1936) served as the 31st vice president of the United States from 1929 to 1933 under Herbert Hoover. Curtis, a Kaw Indian from North Topeka, also held office in both the U.S. House of Representatives and the U.S. Senate.

*Charles Curtis*

**Robert Dole** (born 1923) was a U.S. senator from 1969 to 1996 and was the Senate majority leader from 1984 to 1987 and from 1994 to 1996. Dole was the Republican nominee for U.S. president in 1996. He was born in Russell, Kansas.

*Robert Dole*

**Amelia Earhart** (1897–1937), from Atchison, Kansas, was a famous aviator. In 1932 Earhart became the first woman to fly solo across the Atlantic Ocean. In 1937 Earhart and her navigator disappeared in the Pacific while attempting to fly around the world.

**Dwight D. Eisenhower** (1890–1969) commanded the invasion of Normandy in France, which led to the end of World War II. In 1952 Eisenhower, who grew up in Abilene, was elected the 34th president of the United States.

*Amelia Earhart*

**Maurice Greene** (born 1974) is known as the world's fastest human. The sprinter set a world record in the 100-meter dash in 1999. He won gold medals in the 100-meter dash and the 4 x 100-meter relay in the 2000 Summer Olympics. Greene is from Kansas City.

**Emanuel Haldeman-Julius** (1889-1951) founded the Haldeman-Julius Publishing Company in Girard, Kansas. In 1919 the company began to publish the popular reprint series Little Blue Books, which sold millions of copies and became one of the most successful publishing ventures in U.S. history.

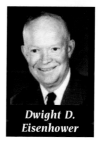

*Dwight D. Eisenhower*

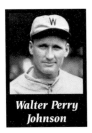

**Walter Perry Johnson**

**Walter Perry Johnson** (1887–1946) was a baseball player born in Humboldt, Kansas. A pitcher and manager for the Washington Senators, Johnson was one of the first players to be named to the Baseball Hall of Fame.

**Buster Keaton** (1895–1966), from Piqua, Kansas, is considered one of the greatest comic actors in film history. Using acrobatic skills he developed as a child, Keaton starred in many silent movies. His most well-known film is *The General*.

**Hattie McDaniel**

**Elmer Verner McCollum** (1879–1967), a chemist and nutritionist, discovered vitamins A, B, D, and E in the early 1900s. McCollum was born in Fort Scott, Kansas.

**Hattie McDaniel** (1895–1952), from Wichita, was the first African American to win an Academy Award. McDaniel won an Oscar for best supporting actress for her role as Mammy in the 1939 film *Gone With the Wind*.

**Carry Nation**

**Carry Nation** (1846–1911), from Garrard County, was a strong supporter of a Kansas law banning the sale of alcohol. She was arrested several times for using a hatchet to smash up saloons where drinks were sold illegally.

**Charlie "Yardbird" Parker** (1920–1955) was a master of the jazz saxophone. He helped to create a fast style of jazz known as bebop. His saxophone playing greatly influenced later musicians. Parker was born in Kansas City, Kansas.

**Charlie "Yardbird" Parker**

**Gordon Parks** (born 1912) is a well-known writer, photographer, and motion-picture producer and director. Parks, from Fort Scott, Kansas, won a Pulitzer Prize for photography in 1973.

**Barry Sanders** (born 1968), a famous football player, grew up in Wichita. After receiving the Heisman Trophy while playing for Oklahoma State University, Barry played with the Detroit Lions, where he was selected to nine consecutive Pro Bowls. In 1998 he announced his retirement.

*Barry Sanders*

**Gale Sayers** (born 1943), of Wichita, was a star running back for the Chicago Bears from 1965 to 1971. He was named to the Pro Football Hall of Fame in 1977.

*Gale Sayers*

**Marilynn Smith** (born 1929) helped found the Ladies Professional Golf Association (LPGA). She was president of the LPGA from 1958 until 1960. Since her retirement from professional golf, she has taught the sport and organizes charity events. Born in Topeka, Kansas, Smith is a member of the Kansas Golf Hall of Fame.

**Russell Stover** (1888–1954) was a businessman from Alton, Kansas. While working as a candymaker, he perfected the Eskimo Pie ice cream treat in 1921. Stover and his wife, Clara, later established Russell Stover Candies, one of the largest boxed-candy companies in the country.

*Russell Stover*

**Vivian Vance** (1909–1979), an actress, was best known for her role as Lucy's friend Ethel Mertz on the 1950s television show "I Love Lucy." She was born in Cherryvale, Kansas.

**Lynette Woodward** (born 1959), a basketball player from Wichita, helped the U.S. women's basketball team win a gold medal in the 1984 Olympic Games. In 1985 Woodward became the first female member of the Harlem Globetrotters. Woodward retired from basketball in 1995 to join the first Wall Street brokerage firm owned by African American women.

*Vivian Vance*

# FACTS-AT-A-GLANCE

**Nickname:** Sunflower State

**Song:** "Home on the Range"

**Motto:** *Ad Astra per Aspera* (To the Stars Through Difficulties)

**Flower:** sunflower

**Tree:** cottonwood

**Bird:** western meadowlark

**Animal:** American buffalo

**Insect:** honeybee

**Reptile:** ornate box turtle

**Date and ranking of statehood:** January 29, 1861, the 34th state

**Capital:** Topeka

**Area:** 82,282 square miles

**Rank in area, nationwide:** 13th

**Average January temperature:** 30° F

**Average July temperature:** 78° F

Kansas adopted its flag in 1927. A wreath above the state seal represents the Louisiana Purchase. The sunflower above the wreath is the state flower.

# POPULATION GROWTH

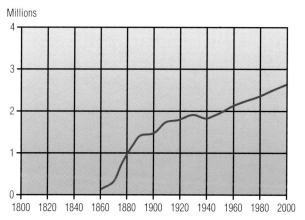

Millions

This chart shows how Kansas's population has grown from 1860 to 2000.

The state seal, adopted in 1861, tells Kansas's history. The 34 stars represent Kansas, the 34th state. The covered wagons represent the journeys of the pioneers. The farmer plowing a field and the barn stand for agriculture. And the Latin words *Ad Astra per Aspera* (To the Stars Through Difficulties) refer to Kansas's troubled times before becoming a state.

**Population:** 2,688,418 (2000 census)

**Rank in population, nationwide:** 32nd

**Major cities and populations:** (2000 census) Wichita (344,284), Overland Park (149,080), Kansas City (146,866), Topeka (122,377), Olathe (92,962)

**U.S. senators:** 2

**U.S. representatives:** 4

**Electoral votes:** 6

**Natural resources:** clays, coal, gravel, natural gas, sand, soil, stone

**Agricultural products:** beef cattle, corn, hay, hogs, sorghum, soybeans, sugar beets, wheat

**Mining:** gypsum, helium, limestone, natural gas, petroleum, salt

**Manufactured goods:** aircraft, aircraft parts, chemicals, coal, food products, machinery, paper products, passenger cars, petroleum products, printed materials, railroad cars and parts, snowplows, trailers

# WHERE KANSANS WORK

**Services**—59 percent (services include jobs in trade; community, social, and personal services; finance, insurance, and real estate; transportation, communication, and utilities)

**Government**—16 percent

**Manufacturing**—13 percent

**Agriculture**—6 percent

**Construction**—5 percent

**Mining**—1 percent

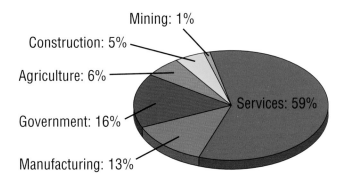

# GROSS STATE PRODUCT

**Services**—57 percent

**Manufacturing**—19 percent

**Government**—13 percent

**Agriculture**—5 percent

**Construction**—4 percent

**Mining**—2 percent

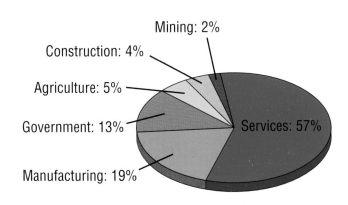

# KANSAS WILDLIFE

**Mammals:** American buffalo, antelope, beaver, black bear, bobcat, coyote, gray fox, grizzly bear, prairie dog, raccoon

**Birds:** bald eagle, black-capped vireo, blue jay, least tern, meadowlark, peregrine falcon, prairie chicken, whooping crane

**Amphibians and reptiles:** American toad, cave salamander, copperhead, cottonmouth, Eastern racer, prairie kingsnake, prairie lizard, red-spotted toad, spotted chorus frog, Texas Horned Lizard

**Fish:** Arkansas River shiner, flathead catfish, largemouth bass, pallid sturgeon, rainbow trout, sicklefin chub, speckled chub, walleye

**Trees:** ash, cottonwood, elm, hackberry, hickory, oak, red cedar, sycamore, walnut, willow

**Wild plants:** asters, bluestem, Dutchman's breeches, Easter daisies, May apples, Mead's milkweed, running buffalo clover, sunflower, sweet William, western prairie fringed orchid

Gray fox

# PLACES TO VISIT

### Boot Hill Museum & Front Street, Dodge City

This outdoor museum re-creates the city's main street as it looked in the 1870s. Special exhibits give the history of the real Dodge City and show what it was like in the Old West.

### Cheyenne Bottoms Wildlife Refuge, Great Bend

The most important ecosystem in Kansas, this refuge is also the most important migration point for shorebirds in North America. The spring and fall migration periods offer an opportunity to view large numbers of different species in one location.

### Dorothy's House, Liberal

See the original model of Dorothy's house used in the 1939 filming of *The Wizard of Oz*. Wander down the Yellow Brick Road to see Dorothy, the Scarecrow, the Tin Man, and the Cowardly Lion, as well as other Oz memorabilia.

### Exploration Place, Wichita

This science museum offers several hands-on activities, such as a simulated fossil dig and four flight simulators. A display features the plants and animals of a Kansas wetland. At the CyberDome Theatre, visitors can choose, view, and create computer graphics.

Dodge City

### Fort Leavenworth, near Leavenworth

Founded in 1827 as the first permanent white settlement in Kansas, this historical site features the Frontier Army Museum. The museum preserves U.S. Army artifacts used at the fort during Kansas's early settlement.

### Fort Riley, near Junction City

Visitors to the fort can see a cavalry museum and the home of General George A. Custer. Many military artifacts are on display, including a WWII M24 tank and an atomic cannon.

### John Brown Memorial Park, Osawatomie

This park was dedicated in 1910 to preserve the battle site where John Brown and his band fought against proslavery groups. The park features the log cabin John Brown lived in and a statue of him.

### Kansas Cosmosphere and Space Center, Hutchinson

The center features a museum of the American space program, with one of the largest collections of space artifacts in the world.

### Kansas History Center, Topeka

The largest historical museum in the state, the center has art demonstrations, hands-on activities for visitors, and food and music.

### Little House on the Prairie, Independence

This reconstructed log cabin is located near the site where author Laura Ingalls Wilder lived as a child. She described her family's life there in *Little House on the Prairie*. A schoolhouse, post office, and gift shop are also available for visitors.

# ANNUAL EVENTS

International Pancake Race, Liberal—*February–March*

Wichita River Festival—*May*

Flint Hills Rodeo, Strong City—*June*

Dodge City Days—*July*

Kansas City Blues and Jazz Festival—*July*

State Fair, Hutchinson—*September*

Kansas City Spirit Festival—*September*

Chisholm Trail Day Festival and Carousel Rendezvous, Abilene—*October*

Dalton Defender Days, Coffeyville—*October*

St. Lucia Festival, Lindsborg—*December*

# LEARN MORE ABOUT KANSAS

## BOOKS

### General

Fradin, Dennis Brindell, and Judith Bloom Fradin. *Kansas.* Danbury, CT: Children's Press, 1998.

Robinson Masters, Nancy. *Kansas.* Danbury, CT: Children's Press, 1999. For older readers.

Thompson, Kathleen. *Kansas.* New York: Raintree Steck-Vaughn, 1996.

### Special Interest

Johnson, Rebecca L. *A Walk in the Prairie.* Minneapolis, MN: Carolrhoda Books, Inc., 2001. Much of Kansas is covered by prairie much like the one described in this book. Color photographs, sketches, and text introduce readers to life on the prairie.

Kerby, Mona. *Amelia Earhart: Courage in the Sky.* New York: Penguin, 1992. This biography recounts the life and mysterious death of the first woman to fly a plane across the Atlantic Ocean.

Winner, Cherie. *The Sunflower Family.* Minneapolis, MN: Carolrhoda Books, Inc., 1996. With colorful photographs, this book teaches readers about the sunflower—Kansas's state flower—and related plants.

## Fiction

Baum, L. Frank. *The Wonderful Wizard of Oz.* New York: HarperCollins, 2000. Originally published in 1900, Baum's classic tells the story of Dorothy and her dog, Toto. Swept away from their Kansas home, they find adventure in a strange land called Oz.

Duey, Kathleen. *Willow Chase: Kansas Territory, 1847.* New York: Aladdin, 1997. Traveling across Kansas Territory in 1847, Willow Chase is swept away by a flooded river. Willow must struggle through difficult and dangerous terrain to find her family.

Garretson, Jerri. *Johnny Kaw: The Pioneer Spirit of Kansas.* Manhattan, KS: Ravenstone Press, 1997. Johnny Kaw is Kansas's tall-tale hero. His adventures include flattening the state and digging the bed of the Kansas River.

MacLachlan, Patricia. *Sarah, Plain and Tall.* New York: HarperCollins, 1985. In 1910 a young woman named Sarah agrees to take care of a Kansas farmer and his two children. Although she misses the New England town where she grew up, she soon realizes her home is with her new family.

Wilder, Laura Ingalls. *Little House on the Prairie.* New York: HarperCollins, 1999. Laura and her family leave their house in the Big Woods of Wisconsin and set out for Kansas. The family face hard times and enjoy good times together.

# WEBSITES

**accessKansas**
<http://www.accesskansas.org>
The official website of Kansas features information about the
state's government, historical sites, and history. Includes links to
general state information as well as fun facts.

**Kansas State Historical Society: Research and Collections**
<http://www.kshs.org/research/index.htm>
This website offers information about the state's history, including
links to historical timelines, notable Kansans, and Kansas facts.

**Topeka Capital-Journal**
<http://www.cjonline.com>
The *Topeka Capital-Journal* is the second largest newspaper in
Kansas and covers state government as well as regional news in
23 northeast Kansas counties.

**CyberSpace Farm**
<http://www.cyberspaceag.com>
Learn more about Kansas farms from the experts who live and
work there. This site features puzzles, pictures, and recipes from
the CyberSpace Farm cookbook.

# PRONUNCIATION GUIDE

**Abilene** (AB-uh-leen)

**Arkansas** (AHR-kuhn-saw) or
(ahr-KAN-zuhs)

**Cheyenne** (shy-AN)

**Coronado, Francisco Vasquez de**
(kaw-ruh-NAH-doh, fran-SIHS-koh
BAHS-kayz day)

**Eisenhower, Dwight** (EYE-zihn-
how-ur)

**Mennonite** (MEHN-uh-nyt)

**Osage** (oh-SAYJ)

**Quivira** (kih-VIHR-uh)

**Topeka** (tuh-PEE-kuh)

**Wichita** (WIH-chuh-taw)

# GLOSSARY

**dike:** a wall or dam built to keep a sea or river from overflowing

**drought:** a long period of extreme dryness due to lack of rain or snow

**Dust Bowl:** an area of the Great Plains region that suffered from dry spells and severe dust storms especially during the 1930s

**glacier:** a large body of ice and snow that moves slowly over land

**homesteader:** a person who settled on and agreed to develop land that was given to him or her by the U.S. government under the Homestead Act of 1862. Most homesteading took place in the western United States between 1852 and 1900.

**marshland:** a spongy wetland soaked with water for long periods of time. Marshes are usually treeless; grasses are the main form of vegetation found in marshes.

**migration:** the movements of birds or other animals from one region or climate to another, usually for feeding or breeding

**prairie:** a large area of level or gently rolling grassy land with few trees

**reservoir:** a place where water is collected and stored for later use

**till:** a mixture of clay, sand, and gravel dragged along by a glacier and left behind when the ice melts

# INDEX

# PHOTO ACKNOWLEDGMENTS

Cover photographs by © Philip Gould/CORBIS (both); PresentationMaps.com, pp. 1, 8, 9, 43; © Tom Bean, pp. 2–3, 3, 4 (detail), 6, 7 (detail), 15, 17 (detail), 37 (detail), 49 (detail); © W.A. Banaszewski/Visuals Unlimited, p. 7; © G. Twiest/Visuals Unlimited, p. 10; © Kent and Donna Dannen, pp. 11, 20, 38, 50, 61; © Lynn Stone, pp. 12 (both), 16; Mike Smith, WeatherData, Incorporated, p. 14; Kansas State Historical Society, pp. 17, 18, 28, 31 (inset, right), 67 (top), 68 (second from bottom); © Geoffrey Clements/CORBIS, p. 21; © Darrell Sampson, pp. 22, 37, 46, 47, 51; Independent Picture Service, pp. 23 (both), 66 (second from bottom); © The Wolfe River, Kansas, c. 1859, Albert Bierstadt, Founders Society Purchase, Dexter M. Ferry, Jr. Fund, Photograph © 1987 The Detroit Institue of Arts; Wisconsin Veterans Museum, p. 24 (right); Tim Seeley, pp. 25, 63, 71, 72; National Archives, pp. 26, 31 (inset, left); © Bettmann/CORBIS, pp. 29, 31; Library of Congress, p. 30; Kansas Collection, University of Kansas Libraries, pp. 31 (inset, center), 34, 35 (right); Mennonite Library and Archives, North Newton, Kansas, p. 32; Joseph J. Pennell Collection, Kansas Collection, University of Kansas Libraries, p. 33; Dwight D. Eisenhower Library, pp. 35 (left), 67 (bottom); John Charlton, Kansas Geological Survey, p. 36; James Blank/Root Resources, p. 39; © Bruce Berg/Visuals Unlimited, p. 40; Cessna Aircraft Company, p. 41; © Douglas Kirkland/CORBIS, p. 42; © Vince Streano/CORBIS, p. 44; Lindsborg Chamber of Commerce, p. 45; © Jeff Jacobsen/KUAC, p. 48; © George Lepp/CORBIS, p. 49; Jerg Kroener, p. 53 (top); Karl Grover, Kansas Department of Wildlife and Parks, p. 53 (bottom); © Tim Zurowski/CORBIS, p. 54; © W. Perry Conway/CORBIS, p. 55; Mike Blair, Kansas Department of Wildlife and Parks, p. 56; Stan Wood, Kansas Department of Wildlife and Parks, p. 57; Lucille Sukalo, p. 58; Jack Lindstrom, p. 60; Hollywood Book and Poster Company, pp. 66 (top, second from top), 68 (second from top, bottom), 69 (bottom); Chrysler Corp., p. 66 (bottom); © Andrea Renault/Globe Photos, Inc, p. 67 (second from top); Schlesinger Library, p. 67 (second from bottom); National Baseball Hall of Fame and Museum, Inc., p. 68 (top); © John Barrett/Globe Photos, Inc., p. 69 (top); Chicago Bears, p. 69 (second from top); Russell Stover Candies, p. 69 (second from bottom); Jean Matheny, p. 70 (top); © Joe McDonald/CORBIS, p. 73; © Dave G. Houser/CORBIS, p. 74; Doyen Salsig, p. 80.